Pre-reader

A Zebra's Day

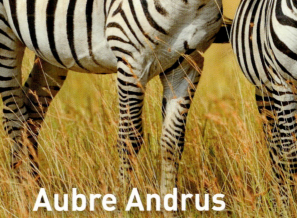

Aubre Andrus

NATIONAL GEOGRAPHIC

Washington, D.C.

Vocabulary Tree

ANIMALS

ZEBRAS

WHAT THEY DO

sip
graze
groom
run

Wake up, zebra.

Look, here's some water!

Stop and sip.

Graze the grass. Yum!

Chomp, chomp.

The zebra grooms its baby.

Now its hair is clean.

The baby's body has stripes.
They are black and white.

No two zebras' stripes look exactly alike!

Stripes make the zebra blend into the grass.

This helps the zebra hide and stay safe.

Watch out! There's a lion!

The zebra calls to its baby.

They run away with their herd.

The baby runs to keep up. Go, baby zebra, go!

Here's some new grass.

Let's eat and rest.

It was a busy day.
Time for the zebra to sleep.

Good night, zebra!

YOUR TURN!

Zebras might look the same, but their stripes are different. A baby zebra must learn who its mother is by looking at her stripes.

Match each zebra to its pattern.

1   2   3

The answer is on the next page.

C

To Mira, my little animal lover —A.A.

The author and publisher gratefully acknowledge the expert content review of this book by Mike McClure, general curator at the Maryland Zoo in Baltimore, and the literacy review of the book by Kimberly Gillow, Principal, Chelsea School District, Michigan.

Copyright © 2020 National Geographic Partners, LLC

Published by National Geographic Partners, LLC, Washington, D.C. 20036. All rights reserved. Reproduction in whole or in part without written permission of the publisher is prohibited.

NATIONAL GEOGRAPHIC and Yellow Border Design are trademarks of the National Geographic Society, used under license.

Designed by Anne LeongSon

Library of Congress Cataloging-in-Publication Data
Names: Andrus, Aubre, author.
Title: A zebra's day / by Aubre Andrus.
Description: Washington, DC : National Geographic Kids, 2020. | Series: National geographic readers | Audience: Ages 2–5 | Audience: Grades K–1
Identifiers: LCCN 2019035891 (print) | LCCN 2019035892 (ebook) | ISBN 9781426337178 (paperback) | ISBN 9781426337185 (library binding) | ISBN 9781426337192 (ebook) | ISBN 9781426337208 (ebook)
Subjects: LCSH: Zebras--Juvenile literature.
Classification: LCC QL737.U62 A754 2020 (print) | LCC QL737.U62 (ebook) | DDC 599.665/7--dc23
LC record available at https://lccn.loc.gov/2019035891
LC ebook record available at https://lccn.loc.gov/2019035892

Photo Credits
Cover, Johan Swanepoel/Shutterstock; 1, byrdyak/Adobe Stock; 2–3, Christopher John Hitchcock/Getty Images; 4–5, pyty/Adobe Stock; 6, Sasha Fenix/Shutterstock; 7, Julian Money-Kyrle/Alamy Stock Photo; 8–9, Cavan for Adobe/Adobe Stock; 10, Jason Edwards/National Geographic Image Collection; 11, simoneemanphoto/Adobe Stock; 12–13, ArCaLu/Shutterstock; 14, MogensTrolle/Getty Images; 15, Four Oaks/Shutterstock; 16–17, Frank Hildebrand/Getty Images; 18–19, BlueOrange Studio/Adobe Stock; 20–21, Anup Shah/Minden Pictures; 22–23, sandsun/Getty Images; 24, Anne LeongSon/NG Staff

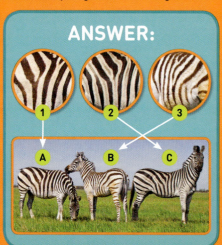

National Geographic supports K–12 educators with ELA Common Core Resources. Visit natgeoed.org/commoncore for more information.

Printed in the United States of America
22/WOR/2 (Paperback)